Welcome to Issue Ten

Check It Out

XTB stands for **eXplore The Bible**.

Read a bit of the Bible each day and...
- Check out <u>who</u> Jesus is and <u>why</u> He came in **John's Gospel**.
- Meet David's son Solomon, and the fiery prophet Elijah, in the books of **1 and 2 Kings**.

Are you ready to explore the Bible? Fill in the bookmark...
...then turn over the page to start exploring with XTB!

 **FOR FAMILIES**

Look out for **Table Talk** — a book to help children and adults explore the Bible together. It can be used by:
- Families
- One adult with one child
- Children's leaders with their groups
- Any other way you want to try

Check it out 10

Table Talk uses the same Bible passages as XTB so that they can be used together if wanted. You can buy Table Talk from your local Christian bookshop—or call us on **0845 225 0880** to order a copy.

T...............

....

Sometimes I'm called

.... **(nickname)**

My birthday is

....

My age is

....

My favourite way to check out what the Bible says is

....

....

How to find your way around the Bible...

Look out for the READ sign.
It tells you what Bible bit to read.

READ
John 20v30-31

So, if the notes say... READ John 20v30-31
...this means chapter 20 and verses 30 to 31
...and this is how you find it.

Use the **Contents** page in your Bible to find where John begins

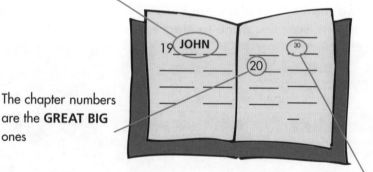

The chapter numbers are the **GREAT BIG** ones

The verse numbers are the tiny ones!

Oops! Keep getting lost?
Cut out this bookmark and use it to keep your place.

How to use 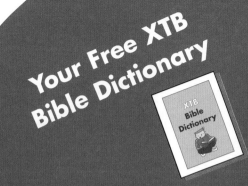xtb

1  Find a time and place when you can read the Bible each day.

2  Get your Bible, a pencil and your XTB notes.

3  Ask God to help you to understand what you read.

4 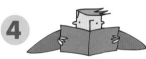 Read today's XTB page and Bible bit.

5  Pray about what you have read and learnt.

6  If you can, talk to an adult or a friend about what you've learnt.

Your Free XTB Bible Dictionary

This copy of XTB comes with a free **XTB Mini Bible Dictionary**.

It will help you check out any odd names or places in your Bible. And it has plenty of maps and pics so that you can see for yourself what things were like in Bible times.

Don't worry if you lose your Bible Dictionary—you'll find a copy of all the words inside the back cover.

Are you ready to try out your Bible Dictionary? Then hurry on to Day 1.

JUMP ON WITH JOHN

xtb **The Book of John**

John

Spot the Difference
There are seven to find.

John

Welcome to John's Gospel. The word 'gospel' means 'good news'. John wrote his book to tell us the good news about **Jesus**.

When you read a book, you usually start at the beginning. But we're going to start at the end...

READ
John 20v30-31

John

Why did John write his book? (v31)

Fill in the gaps.

'so that you may

b_____

that **J**_____ is

the Christ (Messiah), the

S_____ of **G**_____,

and that by believing

you may have

l_____ in His

name.'

John

Some of the signposts in 'Spot the Difference' have words on them. *Write the correct word next to each signpost to see what John is telling us.*

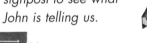

M_____

are like

_____

pointing to

_____

_____ **is.**

John

Miracles are like ***signposts***. They point to <u>who</u> Jesus is, so that we can believe in Him and live with Him for ever in heaven.

In his book, John tells us about many of the miracles that Jesus did. We'll read about some of them in the next few days.

John also tells us many amazing things Jesus <u>said</u>.

John tells us all these things to help us know that Jesus is the **Christ** or **Messiah**.

John

THINK + PRAY

Christ and ***Messiah*** both mean 'God's chosen King'. John's book will help us to find out more about King Jesus and why He came.

Thank God for John's Gospel. Ask Him to help you to learn more about King Jesus as you read John's book, and to believe what you read.

DAY 2 WELL I NEVER!

In today's story, Jesus is on His way from **Judea** to **Galilee**. On the way, He stops off in **Sychar**, a town in **Samaria**.

 Get the hang of the geography by checking out the map in your XTB Bible Dictionary. Look up **'SYCHAR'**.

Did you know?

The people living in Samaria were called **Samaritans**. Jews and Samaritans <u>hated</u> each other. Jews believed that talking to a Samaritan made them unfit for God!

But check out what Jesus does...

READ
John 4v1-7

Where did Jesus stop to rest? (v5-6)

By Jacob's **w**_____ outside the town of **S**_____

What kind of woman did Jesus meet? (v7)
a) A Jew
b) A Samaritan
c) A Martian

 John 4v1-7

Write Jesus' words (v7) in the speech bubble.

Jews didn't talk to <u>Samaritans</u>. But **Jesus** did!
Jewish teachers (Rabbis) didn't talk to <u>women</u>. But **Jesus** did!

 In chapter 3 of John's book, Jesus talked to a Jewish religious leader called Nicodemus. Now Jesus is talking to a nameless Samaritan woman. Jesus talked to <u>both</u> of them about <u>Himself</u> (as we'll see tomorrow). The great news about Jesus is for EVERYONE! It's for Jews, Samaritans, men, women, me... and you!

PRAY Thank God that the great news about Jesus is for everyone—including **you**, and people you don't like to talk to!

DAY 3 LIVING WATER

Yesterday, we found out that <u>Jews</u> didn't talk to <u>Samaritans</u>. But **Jesus** did! He really surprised the Samaritan woman...

> You are a Jew and I am a Samaritan. How can you ask me for a drink?

Jesus' answer was about **water**—but not the kind of water that comes from a well...

READ
John 4v7-14

What kind of water was Jesus talking about? (v10)

L_____ **water**

The woman was puzzled. She knew Jesus didn't have a bucket with Him to get water from the well.

Fill in the missing letters to find out more about this **'living water'**.

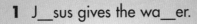

1 J__sus gives the wa__er.

2 It __nds thi__st.

3 It __ever runs out at __ll.

4 It's __ike a __iving water

   spring __nside of you.

5 It gives everlasting li__ __.

Now copy those <u>same letters</u> into the boxes below.

Wow! Jesus is offering this woman **eternal life**—welling up inside her like a bubbling spring! What a fantastic offer!

THINK + PRAY

Eternal life isn't just life for ever. It's knowing Jesus as our Friend and King <u>now</u> so that one day we will live with Him for ever. It's for <u>everyone</u> who believes and trusts in Jesus—the only One who can give it.

If you are a Christian (a follower of Jesus) then you already have His fantastic gift of eternal life. Thank Him for it now.

DAY 4 — WHO IS JESUS?

Jesus has offered 'living water' to the Samaritan woman. He is offering her eternal life. But she thinks He means water that will stop her getting thirsty...

READ
John 4v15-19

This woman had never met Jesus before, but He <u>knew</u> all about her! What did she say He was? (v19)

A p_____

 *Look up **PROPHET** in your XTB Bible Dictionary.*

The woman thought Jesus was a messenger from God, so she decided to ask Him a question about <u>where</u> God should be worshipped. (This was something Jews and Samaritans didn't agree about.)

But Jesus had something <u>far</u> more important to tell her...

READ
John 4v19-26

Take the <u>first</u> letter of each pic to see two important things Jesus said.

_____

is from the __ __ __ __ __ (v22)

 *Look up **SALVATION** in your XTB Bible Dictionary.*

Jesus was a <u>Jew</u>. He came to <u>rescue</u> us from sin. (*We'll find out more about this as we keep reading John's Gospel.*)

Jesus is the __ __ __ __ __ __ __

 *Look up **MESSIAH** in your XTB Bible Dictionary.*

Wow! Jesus is the Messiah (Christ). He is God's chosen King, who came to rescue us!

THINK + PRAY

Jesus, <u>God's chosen King</u>, knew this woman wasn't living as God wanted. *Disaster!* Except that He had come to rescue her from her sin. *Fantastic!* What wrong stuff does King Jesus know about <u>you</u>? Thank God for sending Jesus to rescue you from all that.

Who <u>didn't</u> Jews talk to? **S**_____

Who <u>didn't</u> Jewish teachers talk to? **W**_____

Check back to Day 2 if you're not sure.

Jesus' disciples have been off buying food. Now they're back with lunch, and about to get a shock...

READ
John 4v27-30

(Circle) the correct answers.

When the **children/disciples/teachers** returned, they were **amused/pleased/surprised** to see Jesus **talking/singing/playing** with a **woman/man/child**. But they didn't ask why. The woman left her **wheelbarrow/water jar/skateboard** and went back to the **town/mountain/stream**. She said to the people, 'Come and see the man who told me **everything/something/nothing** I ever did. Could he be the Messiah?' They came out of the **hills/houses/town** and went to see Jesus.

Now fit the words you circled into the puzzle. The <u>yellow</u> boxes will spell two new words.

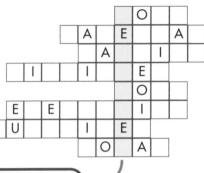

The woman dashed back to town to **tell them** about Jesus. She didn't know much about Jesus yet—but she told them what she knew, and invited them to come and meet Him.

THINK + PRAY

This woman is a great example for us to follow! Maybe you feel you don't know much about Jesus? Don't worry! Just tell your friends what you do know, and invite them to find out more. (*Maybe they could come to church with you? Or you could do XTB together?*) Think of one friend you would like to tell about Jesus. _____

Now ask God to give you a chance to do it!

DAY 6 HARVEST TIME

Feeling hungry? What would be your top choice to eat right now?

The disciples have just turned up with Jesus' lunch. But He has something far more important on His mind...

READ
John 4v31-34

On Day 3 Jesus was talking about **water**—but not the kind you <u>drink</u>. Now He's talking about **food**—but not the kind you <u>eat</u>! What does He say His food is? (v34)

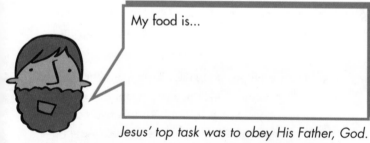

> My food is...

Jesus' top task was to obey His Father, God.

READ
John 4v35-38

Hmm... read on to find out more...

Those verses are a bit tricky. Cross out the **X**s, **Y**s and **Z**s to see the **XTB Xplanation**.

Jesus is talking about the **XHYARZXVYESZTY** of eternal life. That means telling people about **YXJXESYYUZSX**. And those people becoming **ZXCHYRXXISYTZXIAYNSY**.

That's what Jesus was doing when He talked to the Samaritan woman. You can see why chatting to her was loads more important than munching His lunch!

THINK + PRAY

Whose name did you write in yesterday's prayer? _____

If you didn't, go back and do it now!

Have you told them about Jesus yet? If you have, that's great! Thank God for helping you to do it. If you haven't, <u>don't</u> worry—but <u>don't</u> leave it! Plan a time to talk to them—then ask God to help you.

CHECK IT OUT

There's a giant chicken outside— and it's giving away free chocolate!

WoW! I've got to see this for myself!

Katie's news was **amazing**—so Alice went to check it out for herself.

The Samaritan woman had told the people from her town all about Jesus. It was **amazing** news—so the people went to check it out for themselves...

READ
John 4v39-42

What did the people beg Jesus to do? (v40)

S_____ with them

How long did Jesus stay? (v40)   _____ **days**

This meant the Samaritans could hear Jesus for themselves (v42). What did they believe about Him now? (v42)

He really is the

S_____

of the **w**_____

Saviour means **Rescuer.**

Two days ago, we saw that the Samaritan woman told others about Jesus—and that we should do the same.

Now we've seen how the Samaritans checked out what she had told them. Again, we should do the same...

When you hear a talk in church, or read something in XTB, how do you know it's true? Whenever possible, you should check it out for yourself in the **Bible**.

Dear XTB Reader,
When I write XTB, I try very hard to only write things that are true. But I'm not perfect, and I might make mistakes! So please <u>always</u> check what I've written. Look up the Bible verses, and see for yourself what they say. Check that I've got it right. Thanks!

Alison

PRAY

Pray for the people who teach you the Bible. Ask God to help <u>them</u> to teach it correctly, and ask Him to help <u>you</u> to check it out for yourself.

Today's story starts in the town of **Cana**, in Galilee.

*Look up **CANA** in your XTB Bible Dictionary.*

How far was it from Cana to Capernaum? _____ **miles**

In Capernaum, a boy was lying in bed, very ill

Meanwhile, in Cana, the boy's father had gone to see Jesus.

Please come and help my son!

It was one o'clock in the afternoon.

Go home. Your son will live.

The man took Jesus at His word, and set off for home...

Stop the story for a moment!
How do you think the father <u>felt</u>, as he hurried home 20 miles to see his son?
(Circle) your answers, then add two more of your own.

hopeful   worried   trusting   scared

Now read the whole story for yourself...

READ
John 4v46-54

Did the man's son get better? (v51) **Yes / No**

What time did he get better? (v52)

Note: The 'seventh hour' in Jewish time-keeping means 'one o'clock in the afternoon'.

THINK + PRAY

Read verse 50 again.
The father didn't wait for proof. He took Jesus at His word. That's what **faith** is. Faith isn't a feeling. It means **believing** that what God says in the Bible is true.
Do <u>you</u> believe God's words in the Bible?

YES
Faith is a gift from God. Thank Him for helping you to believe.

NOT SURE
Ask God to help you to believe.

DAY 9 MAT MATTERS

xtb John 5v1-9

Today's story happened in Jerusalem, at a pool near the Sheep Gate. (Baa!)

*Look up **SHEEP GATE POOL** in your XTB Bible Dictionary.*

The pool looked like this.

When Jesus went to the pool, He met a man who hadn't been able to walk for a very l-o-n-g time...

READ
John 5v1-6

How long had the man been ill? (v5) **28/38/48** years

Fill in what Jesus asked him (v6).

Do you...

Think what the man might have said—then **read it** for yourself in the verses.

READ
John 5v7-9

The man gave a very grumbly answer, didn't he! Did Jesus still heal him? (v9) **Yes / No**

This man couldn't make himself better. He couldn't even get himself into the pool! Who was the only person who could heal him?

What was your answer? Did you write Jesus? Or God? Both of those answers are right! *Copy all the red letters (in order) to find out why.*

— — — — — — — — — — — —

THINK + PRAY

*Look up **MIRACLES** in your XTB Bible Dictionary. This miracle was another signpost pointing to who Jesus is. Only God could heal this man—but Jesus **is** God! So... Do you trust Him? ...listen to Him? ...obey Him? ...love Him?*

DAY 10 MISSING THE POINT

xtb John 5v10-16

Jesus had just healed a man who had been ill for **38** years! If <u>you</u> were there, what would you say to that man?

Draw your face here, and fill in the speech bubble.

This all happened on the **Sabbath**.

Look up **SABBATH** *in your XTB Bible Dictionary.*

Some of the Jewish religious leaders saw the man who had been healed...

READ
John 5v10-16

What did the Jewish leaders say? (v10)
✔ *Tick the correct speech bubble, and <u>draw</u> their faces.*

> Who healed you? He must be very special!

> It's great that you can walk again!

> Stop carrying your mat! It's against the rules!

The religious leaders should have been <u>thrilled</u> that this man was better. But instead, they were <u>cross</u> because he was carrying a mat! They completely ***missed the point.***

Yesterday we saw that this miracle was like a **signpost**, showing us that Jesus is God. But the Jewish leaders missed that point as well! What did they decide to do? (v16)

a) Spend time with Jesus to find out more about who He was.

b) Persecute Jesus (give Him a hard time) because He broke their Sabbath rules.

c) Go to McDonalds.

More about their decision tomorrow...

PRAY

It's great that you're reading John's book about Jesus. Ask God to help you to understand what you read, so that you don't miss the point about who Jesus is and how to follow Him.

Jesus healed a man who had been ill for 38 years. **Yippee!** But the Jewish leaders got cross because the man was carrying a mat on the Sabbath! **Uh-oh...**

They'd completely missed the point about who Jesus is—so Jesus made it extra clear to them...

READ
John 5v17

What did Jesus say? (v17)

> My **F**_____ is always working, and I too must **w**_____.

Use the **arrow code** to see what this means.

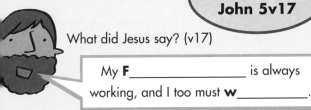

Arrow Code
⇧ = A
⬈ = B
⬊ = D
⇩ = E
⬈ = F
⇦ = G
⬂ = H
➡ = K
⬅ = O
◁ = R
▷ = S
△ = T
◁ = W

Wow! Jesus is saying that He is God's <u>Son</u>, and does the same work that His Father does. That's fantastic! But the Jewish leaders didn't think so...

READ
John 5v18

What did the Jewish leaders decide to do? (v18)

K_____ Jesus

THINK + PRAY

When the Jewish leaders heard Jesus say that God was His Father, they refused to believe it. What do <u>you</u> think?

a) I think it might be true. I'd like to find out more about Jesus.

b) I believe it's true. I'd like to tell my friends about Jesus.

c) _____

Talk to God about your answer. If you need God's help, ask Him for it now.

DAY 12 HONOUR JESUS

 John 5v19-23

Jesus is talking about the most important person in the world: **Himself!** Let's listen in on what He says...

READ
John 5v19-23

Hmm... there's some tricky stuff in there. Take the first letter of each pic to see the **XTB Xplanation**.

Jesus does what __ __ __ **does.** (v19)

God shows Jesus His __ __ __ __ __ . (v20)

Jesus has power to give __ __ __ __ . (v21)

God gives Jesus the right to __ __ __ __ __ .
(v22)

Wow! What do these verses say about Jesus?
a) Jesus is a little bit important.
b) Jesus is almost as important as the American President.
c) Jesus is the most important person in the world.

 What does v23 say we must do?

H_____
Jesus (the Son)

THINK SPOT

How will <u>you</u> honour Jesus (show Him love and respect) this week? (*eg: tell Him how great He is, live in a way that pleases Him, tell others about Him...*)

PRAY Ask God to help you do these things. You can start now!

Spot **six** differences between the pics.

Yesterday we saw that **Jesus** is our **Judge**. Jesus explains what that means in the next few verses. Look out for the words *judge*, *judged*, and *judgement* as you read them.

READ
John 5v24-30

They're still a bit tricky aren't they??? Verse 27 tells us that *God* gives Jesus the right to be our Judge, and v30 says that Jesus' judgement is always *right*.

Does it matter?

- At a <u>dog show</u>, the judge chooses the best dog. There's a prize for winning, but it's not too important.
- In <u>court</u>, the judge decides what punishment to give. Someone may go to prison, or be set free. That's pretty important!
- But when **Jesus** judges us, He decides if we live <u>with</u> Him for ever in heaven, or <u>without</u> Him for ever. That's totally important!!!

Fill in the gaps from v24.

Whoever **h**_____ my words and **b**_____ Him who sent me has **e**_____ life.

These are some of the most important words in John's Gospel. *Turn to 'Judge and Rescuer' on the next page to find out more.*

THINK SPOT

Time to Think
- Are you a follower of Jesus?
- Do you want to be? (*Go back to **Judge and Rescuer** if you're not sure.*)
- Do you want to tell your friends about Jesus?

PRAY Talk to God about your answers. Ask Him to help you.

JUDGE AND RESCUER

JESUS IS OUR JUDGE

God has given Jesus the right to be our <u>Judge</u> (v27). **But there's a problem!** We are all <u>guilty</u> (have to be punished)—because we all <u>sin</u>.

What is Sin?

Sin is more than just doing wrong things. We all like to be in charge of our own lives. We do what **we** want instead of what **God** wants. This is called **sin**.

Sin gets in the way between us and God. It stops us from knowing Him and stops us from being His friends.

Because we all sin, we are all **guilty**, and deserve to be punished.

Write GUILTY under the picture.

JESUS IS OUR RESCUER

But the great news is that Jesus came to **rescue** us from our sins!

How did Jesus rescue us?

At the first Easter, when Jesus was about 33 years old, He was crucified. He was nailed to a cross and left to die.

As He died, all the sins of the world (all the wrongs people do) were put onto Jesus, so that God punished <u>Him</u>! Jesus took all our sin and all the punishment we deserve. He died in our place, as our Rescuer, so that we can be forgiven.

Did you know?

Jesus died on the cross as our Rescuer—but He didn't stay dead! After three days God brought Him back to life! Jesus is still alive today, ruling as our King.

If we <u>believe</u> in Jesus, and come to Him to be forgiven, then we are judged **Not Guilty** and won't be punished (v24).

Write NOT GUILTY under the picture.

If we put our trust in Jesus as our **Rescuer**, we will be judged <u>Not Guilty</u> by Jesus as our **Judge**—and one day live in heaven with Him for ever.

Have YOU been rescued by Jesus? Turn to the next page to find out more...

AM I A CHRISTIAN?

Not sure if you're a Christian? Then check it out below...

Christians are people who have been rescued by Jesus and follow Him as their King.

You can't become a Christian by trying to be good.

That's great news, since you can't be totally good all the time!

It's about accepting what Jesus did on the cross to rescue you. To do that, you will need to **ABCD**.

A **Admit** your sin—that you do, say and think wrong things. Tell God you are sorry. Ask Him to forgive you, and to help you to change. There will be some wrong things you have to stop doing.

B **Believe** that Jesus died for you, to take the punishment for your sin; that He came back to life, and that He is still alive today.

C **Consider** the cost of living like God's friend from now on, with Him in charge. It won't be easy. Ask God to help you do this.

D **Do** something about it! In the past you've gone your own way rather than God's way. Will you hand control of your life over to Him from now on? If you're ready to ABCD, then talk to God now. The prayer will help you.

A prayer

Dear God,
I have done and said and thought things that are wrong. I am really sorry. Please forgive me. Thank you for sending Jesus to die for me. From now on, please help me to live as one of Your friends, with You in charge.   Amen

Jesus welcomes <u>everyone</u> who comes to Him. If you have put your trust in Him, He has rescued you from your sins and will help you to live for Him. That's great news!

DAY 14 — THE WITNESSES

*Look up **JESUS** in your XTB Bible Dictionary.*

What does the name **Jesus** mean? **G_____ S_____**

In the last few days we've seen that Jesus is **God** (Day 9) and that He came to **save** us (Day 13). But the Jewish leaders didn't believe it—so Jesus told them about the **witnesses**... *(see XTB Dictionary)*

READ
John 5v31-35

Who is Jesus talking about? (v33) **J_____**

This is **John the Baptist** (<u>not</u> the John who wrote the Gospel).

*Cross out the **X**'s to see what John said about Jesus.*

There is the **XXLXAMXBXX** of God, who takes away the **XXSXIXXNX** of the **XWOXXRXLXDXX**. John 1v29

READ
John 5v36

Do you remember what Jesus' **miracles** are like?

S_____

Check your XTB Dictionary if you're not sure.

The amazing things Jesus did were like **signposts**. They showed that He had been sent by God (v36).

READ
John 5v37-40

What did the Jewish leaders study? (v39)

The S_____

The Scriptures are the Old Testament part of the Bible. The Old T is full of promises about **Jesus**—but the Jewish leaders hadn't spotted them! (*We'll see some examples tomorrow...*)

THINK SPOT

Do some of your friends think that believing in Jesus is silly? It's not! We have loads of good evidence that Jesus really is who He says He is —the Son of God. If you can, ask an older Christian to show you some of it.

PRAY

Getting stuck in to the Bible is the best way to learn more about Jesus. But you don't want to be like those Jewish leaders!—so ask God to help you understand and believe what you read.

DAY 15 MOSES SUPPOSES

John 5v41-47

QUICK QUIZ

Four facts about **Moses**. Are they **True** (T) or **False** (F) ?

a) The name Moses means 'saved from the water'. T / F

b) Moses had a brother called Airy. T / F

c) Moses led the Israelites out of Egypt. T / F

d) Moses wrote the last five books of the Old T. T / F

Now check your answers by looking up
MOSES *in your XTB Bible Dictionary.*

The Jewish leaders were big fans of Moses. He wrote the first five books of the Old T, and they knew those books back to front! **BUT** Jesus told the Jewish leaders off, because they didn't believe in Him (v41-44)—and then Jesus told them that Moses had written all about Him!!!

READ
John 5v45-47

Fill in the gaps from v46.

If you believed **M_____**, you would believe **m___**, because he **w_____** about me.

Time to check out some things Moses wrote about Jesus...

READ
Genesis 49v10

A *sceptre* is a pole carried by a king. This verse says that someone from Judah's family would be <u>king for ever</u>. That king is **Jesus**!

READ
Deuteronomy 18v15

God promised that He would send a *prophet* (God's messenger) like Moses. This new prophet was **Jesus**!

The Jewish leaders knew the Old T really well, but <u>didn't</u> see that so much of it points to Jesus! In chapter 6 we'll find that the crowds <u>do</u> see that Jesus is the prophet like Moses. *More about that on Day 42.*

THINK + PRAY

We'll come back to John's Gospel on Day 41. But for now, think back over the things you've learnt about Jesus in chapters 4 and 5. (Flick back through the headings in your Bible.) What do you want to thank Jesus for?

GOOD KING BAD KING

Welcome to the book of 1 Kings!

What do you think it's about?

a) Kings
b) Queens
c) Playing cards

No, it's not a trick question!
1 Kings is all about the <u>kings</u> of Israel.
So is the book that comes after it, called
2 Kings.

These books tell us about the kings who came after King David. There was a gaggle of good kings, and a bunch of bad kings!

Use the Crown Code to see what made a king good or bad...

Crown Code

👑 = B
👑 = D
👑 = E
👑 = G
👑 = H
👑 = I
👑 = L
👑 = N
👑 = O
👑 = P
👑 = R
👑 = S
👑 = T
👑 = V
👑 = Y

GOOD KINGS

- _ _ _ _ _ _ _ and _ _ _ _ _ _ _ _ God.

- Listened to God's messengers, the _ _ _ _ _ _ _ _ _ .

- Helped their _ _ _ _ _ _ _ to live for God.

BAD KINGS

- _ _ _ _ _ _ _ _ _ _ _ God.

- _ _ _ _ _ _ _ _ the prophets.

- Prayed to _ _ _ _ _ _ _ _ gods (statues), and led their people to pray to pretend gods too.

Find out more on the next page.

WALKING IN HIS WAYS

xtb 1 Kings 2v1-4

David had been a <u>good</u> king. Before he died, David told his son **Solomon** how he could be a good king too...

READ
1 Kings 2v1-4

What did David tell Solomon to do? (v3)
- **a)** Disobey God's laws.
- **b)** Obey God's laws.
- **c)** Change God's laws.

Some Bible versions say **'Walk in his ways'** in verse 3. This means to love God and obey His laws.

If Solomon, and the kings who came after him, walked in God's ways, then someone from David's family would always be king of Israel (v4).

Would Solomon and co. do this???
We'll find out as we read 1 Kings.

I'm not a king or queen—and I guess you're not either! But God still calls us to **walk in His ways**.

Circle the things this means for you.

Not fighting with your brother or sister.

Obeying your parents straight away.

Gossiping

Always telling the truth.

Doing handstands

Reading the Bible.

Praying   Bullying   Grumbling   Sharing

THINK + PRAY

Are you living the way God wants you to? What makes it hard for you to obey God? If you want to walk in God's ways, tell Him the things you find hard, and then ask Him to help you. He will!

DAY 17 SOLOMON'S CHOICE

Have you ever read a story where someone is given three wishes? Today's true story from the Bible is a bit like that—except it's REAL! The wonderful God of the universe really did offer to give Solomon anything he wanted!

READ
1 Kings 3v5

God spoke to Solomon in a dream. Copy His words into the speech bubble.

 THINK SPOT

What would _you_ ask for?

Now read Solomon's answer...

READ
1 Kings 3v6-15

What did Solomon ask? (v9)

right   wisdom   wrong

Give me the **w**_____

I need to rule your people and to know the difference between

r_____ and **w**_____.

How did God feel about Solomon's answer? (v10)

God was p_____

Did God give Solomon the wisdom he asked for? (v12) **Yes / No**

What else did God give Solomon? (v13)

THINK + PRAY

Wow! Look how generous God is! Not only did He give Solomon more wisdom than anyone had ever had, but He gave him riches and honour as well! When _you_ are praying, this is the wonderful generous God you are praying to. Pray to Him now, and thank Him for His generosity.

DAY 18 HOW TO PRAY

1 Kings 3v6-9

Write down three things you can remember praying about recently.

1. _____

2. _____

3. _____

Sometimes, praying feels **easy**:
- if we're excited about something God has done, it's easy to <u>thank</u> Him;
- or if we have a problem, we'll want to ask for God's <u>help</u>.

But sometimes praying is really **hard**, and we can't think what to say.

Read Solomon's prayer again from yesterday's story.

READ
1 Kings 3v6-9

This prayer gives a great pattern to follow. *Take the first letter of each pic to see what it is.* ↓

_ _ _ _ _ _ _ _ _ _ God for His _ _ _ _ _ _ _ _

Solomon thanked God for being so kind to his father David (v6).
Think: What can <u>you</u> thank God for?

_ _ _ _ _ _ _ _ _ God for keeping His _ _ _ _ _ _ _ _

The Israelites had become *'a great people, too many to count or number'* (v8).
This is what God had promised to Abraham 1000 years earlier.
Think: What promise do <u>you</u> want to praise God for?

_ _ _ _ _ _ _ _ for the good of God's _ _ _ _ _ _ _

Solomon knew that the Israelites needed a good king, who would rule them wisely.
He asked for wisdom for <u>their</u> sake, rather than his own (v9).
Think of some of God's people today (*eg: Christians from your church, or school, or in your family*). What do you want to pray for them?

PRAY Now spend time praying in these three ways. And remember what we learnt yesterday—that God <u>loves</u> to give generous answers.

DAY 19 ONE BABY—TWO MUMS!

Solomon had asked God for **wisdom**. Now it was time to use it...

Two women, who lived in the same house, both had babies.

During the night, one of the babies died.

But the woman whose baby died swapped her dead baby for the living one!

In the morning, when the other woman woke up, she found a dead baby beside her.

But it wasn't <u>her</u> baby!

The women argued about it—so they went to see Solomon.

The living baby is mine! No—it's mine!

Solomon found a wise way to settle their argument.
Bring me a sword.

Now cut the living child in half, and give half to each woman.

What a shocking thing for Solomon to suggest! *Read the passage to find out what happened.*

READ 1 Kings 3v24-28

Did Solomon work out who the real mum was? (v27) **Yes / No**

Based on 1 Kings 3v16-25

Solomon had more wisdom than anyone else, and all the Israelites were filled with deep respect for him (v28). But even so, Solomon was nothing like as wise or good as the 'King of Kings'. *Copy the letters hidden in the cartoon story (in order) to see who that is.*

— — — — — — — — —

PRAY King Jesus is our perfect, wise Ruler. He always does and says what's right. He always knows the best way for us to live, and will show us if we ask Him. Ask King Jesus to show you, through the Bible, the wisest way to live. And if anything is worrying you, ask Jesus to show you the wise answer to it.

DAY 20 LOTS AND LOTS

1 Kings 4v1-19 lists <u>lots</u> of people. They have great names like **Zadok**, **Ben-Deker** and **Jehoshaphat!**

Scan the lists and choose your <u>favourite</u> name. What is it?

Solomon ruled Israel wisely, just as God said he would. These men helped Solomon to do it.

In verse 20 there's <u>lots</u> of something else as well...

READ
1 Kings 4v20

Fill in the gaps.

This means all of the Israelites.

> The people of (Judah and Israel) were as numerous as the
> **s**_____ on the **s**_____;
> they **a**_____, they **d**_____
> and they were **h**_____.

FLASHBACK!
1000 years earlier, God made a promise to **Abraham**.

READ
Genesis 22v17-18

Promise One (v17)
Abraham's family (the Israelites) would become too <u>HUGE</u> to count. It would be like trying to count the sand on a beach!
Did God keep that promise?   **Yes / No**

Promise Two (v18)
Someone from Abraham's family would be God's way of blessing the whole world. God kept that promise too, by sending His Son Jesus (who died for us so that our sins can be forgiven).

PRAY   God <u>always</u> keeps His promises. Thank God that nothing (and no one!) can stop His words coming true.

DAY 21 ⟁ ⟰ ⬇ ⬈⟁⬅⬇⬆⟁⬇ ➡⬇⬇⬈⬇⟁

Use the **Arrow Code** to find the title of today's page.

This is one of my favourite titles for an XTB page, because it reminds me that our wonderful God makes and keeps promises to His people.

We read about <u>one</u> of those promises yesterday. Now use the code again to discover <u>two</u> more...

1

God promised to give Abraham's family (the

⬈ ⬆ ⬈ ⬊

Israelites) all of the __ __ __ __ from the border of Egypt across to the great river Euphrates. (*This promise is in Genesis 15v18.*)

2

God promised David that the Israelites would

⬈ ⬇ ⬆ ⬅ ⬇

have __ __ __ __ __ from their enemies. (*This promise is in 2 Samuel 7v10-11.*)

Now read the next chunk of 1 Kings—(it's all about Solomon's rule as king)—and look out for clues that these two promises had come true.

READ
1 Kings 4v21-28

Arrow Code	
⇧	= A
⇨	= C
⬊	= D
⬇	= E
⬋	= H
⬆	= I
➡	= K
⬊	= L
⬇	= M
⬈	= N
⬅	= O
⬉	= P
◁	= R
▷	= S
△	= T
◁	= W

A Which verses show that the Israelites were living in the **land** God had promised them?

v_____ & v_____

B Which verses shows that the Israelites had the **peace** God had promised them?

v_____ & v_____

Check your answers at the bottom of the page.

Do you have a favourite promise from the Bible?

(*If you're not sure, check out **PROMISES** in your XTB Bible Dictionary.*)

PRAY Thank God for the promise you chose. Ask Him to help you to trust Him to keep <u>all</u> His promises.

DAY 22 WISE, WISER, WISEST

 xtb 1 Kings 4v29-34

Use yesterday's Arrow Code.

◁ ↑ ▷ ⬃ ← ↓

Today's verses are about Solomon's _ _ _ _ _ _.

As you read the passage, put a **'W'** in the box each time you read **wisdom**, **wise**, **wiser** or **wisest**.

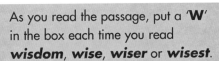

READ
1 Kings 4v29-34

How many **W**s did you put in the box?

Solomon's wisdom was amazing! Verse 29 tells us why.

Because G_____ gave it to him.

(Circle) some of the things Solomon knew about (v33).

It sounds like Solomon loved using his wisdom to find out about God's fantastic world, and then tell others about it too.

Choose something that God has made, and examine it closely (like Solomon did). It might be a flower (in the garden?), an animal (your pet hamster?) or even your own hand! Draw it or describe it here.

PRAY

Now praise God for His wonderful handiwork.

XTB Challenge: Today (or tomorrow if you read XTB at bedtime) spot as many things as possible that God has made. Thank Him for each one of them.

DAY 23 ONLY THE BEST

1 Kings 5&6

FLASHBACK!

Solomon's dad, David, had wanted to build a temple for God. But God told David it wasn't <u>his</u> job to build a temple —it would be his son's job to do it.

In his fourth year as king, Solomon started to build the temple. *Use the Circle Code to see what he made it of.*

_ _ _ _ _

The walls and floors and ceilings were made of beautiful cedar wood. The wood came from Hiram, the king of Tyre. His men cut the logs and floated them down the sea in rafts to where Solomon wanted them. (1 Kings 5v8-9)

_ _ _ _ _

Large blocks of top quality stone were cut from a quarry. The stone was shaped <u>before</u> it was brought to the temple so that there was no sound of hammering or cutting in the temple as it was being built. (1 Kings 6v7)

_ _ _ _

The whole of the inside of the temple was covered in pure gold. Even the floors were gold! (1 Kings 6v21&30)

READ
1 Kings 6v37-38

How long did it take to build the temple? (v38) _____ **years**

The temple looked like this. It was about 30 metres long, 10 metres broad and 15 metres high. It was a magnificent building, beautifully decorated, and full of gold.

THINK + PRAY

Solomon had his best craftsmen working on the temple, using the best materials. Only the **best** would do! How can <u>you</u> give your best to God? Think carefully about your answer (it might involve your time, or money, or skills, or...). Now talk to God about it.

DAY 24 THE PROMISE & THE POWER

Chapter 7 of 1 Kings tells us a bit about Solomon's palace, and then <u>loads</u> more about the **temple**.

Look again at the temple picture on the opposite page. Do you see the two huge bronze pillars (or columns) outside the temple? They looked very impressive—but that's <u>not</u> the only reason they were there...

READ
1 Kings 7v21-22

Um??? Why were the pillars given names?

 Check out **Temple Pillars** *in your XTB Bible Dictionary.*

*Now write the **names** on the pillars, and what each name **means**.*

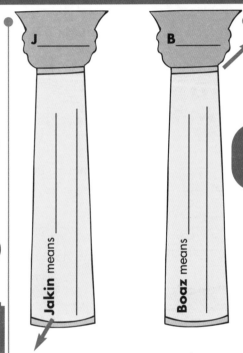

J_____

Jakin means

B_____

Boaz means

God had promised **David** (Solomon's dad) that He would 'establish' his kingdom for ever. That meant that someone from David's family would be king for ever (2 Samuel 7v12-13).

God had the <u>strength</u> to keep His promise about David's family line. And if Solomon (and other kings after him) were to be good kings, they needed to rely on God's <u>strength</u> to help them.

Every time Solomon saw these pillars he would be reminded of **God's promise** and **God's power**.

THINK + PRAY

Write these words on two pieces of paper: **GOD ESTABLISHES** (He makes and keeps promises); **IN GOD IS STRENGTH** (He helps us live for Him). *Stick them on either side of your bedroom door.* Ask God to help you to trust His promises, and rely on His strength.

DAY 25 GOD IS WITH US

Now that the temple was finished, Solomon and co. had a party to celebrate! But first, they had to bring something very important into the temple...

READ
1 Kings 8v1-9

What did the priests carry into the temple? (v6)

The _____

Where did they put it? (v6)

The M_____ **H**_____ **P**_____

Did you know?

The Ark of the Covenant
(The Covenant Box)
The ark was a wooden box, covered in gold. Inside the ark were two stone tablets with the Ten Commandments written on them.

The ark reminded the Israelites of something very important. *Shade in the letters with a <u>dot</u> to see what that was.*

Now that the ark was in the temple, it meant that the <u>temple</u> also reminded the people that **God was with them**.

THINK + PRAY

Since Jesus, God's people don't need a temple. If you are a Christian (a follower of Jesus) then God is with <u>you</u> wherever you are. Jot down some of the places where God is with you (eg: at home, school, up a tree...)

Now thank God that He is with you in all of these places—and everywhere else too!

DAY 26 CROWDED BY A CLOUD!

Do you ever look at the clouds and try to make pictures from their shapes? *Try it now. Turn these clouds into pictures.*

Imagine turning up for a church service, and finding you can't go in because the building is full of cloud! That's what happened at the temple...

READ
1 Kings 8v10-13

What was the cloud a sign of? (v11)
a) The glory of the LORD
b) The LORD's presence
c) It was going to rain

Both a) and b) are right. The cloud was a sign of God's presence. He had completely filled the temple with His glory!

Think of some words to describe a thick cloud.

When a cloud is thick, you can <u>see</u> it, but you can't see <u>through</u> it.

The Israelites could see the cloud, so they knew that God was there—that He was <u>with</u> them. But they couldn't see God Himself.

God is too dazzling and wonderful for a human being to be able to look at Him. (Once, when Moses asked to see God's face, all he saw was a glimpse of God's back. Anything more would have been too much for him! Exodus 33v20-23)

THINK SPOT What's the best way for us to see God? Think carefully, then read the upside down answer in the box.

Jesus told His followers that they could see God by looking at Him (John 14v9). As we read about Jesus in the Bible, He shows us what God is like.

PRAY Ask God to help you to see Him and know Him more and more as you read the Bible.

DAY 27 SOLOMON SPEAKS

The temple was finished. The ark was is in its place. The cloud had filled the temple. Now Solomon had some things to say...

READ
1 Kings 8v14-21

Fill in the missing words.

> **P**_____ the **L**_____ , the God of Israel.
> He has kept the promise he made to my father
> **D**_____. My father planned to build a
> **t**_____ for God, but God told him, 'It is
> your **s**_____ who will build a temple for me.'

> The Lord has kept his **p**_____.
> I have succeeded my father as king.
> I have built the temple for God, and
> provided a place there for the **a**_____.

Now find all of those missing words in the wordsearch.
Some are backwards!

P	E	L	P	M	E	T
R	O	D	A	V	I	D
E	S	I	M	O	R	P
L	O	R	D	M	I	S
S	O	N	A	R	K	E
P	R	A	I	S	E	S

What do the leftover
letters spell (in order)? — — — — — — — —

God kept all of the promises He had made to David and
Solomon! God <u>always</u> keeps His promises.

THINK + PRAY

 *Look up '**PROMISES**' in
your XTB Bible Dictionary.*

Use the words of these promises
to help you to pray to God.

DAY 28 NO ONE LIKE GOD

Think of some words to describe God. Choose at least five.

Today we're going to start reading Solomon's prayer when the temple was dedicated to God. He begins by praising God...

READ
1 Kings 8v22-26

Fill in the gaps from v23.

L _ _ _ God of Israel, there is no g _ _ like you in h _ _ _ _ _ _ above or e _ _ _ _ _ below!

Solomon knows that there's no other god like the God of Israel.

What makes God <u>different</u> from other gods? (v23)

a) He keeps His covenant
b) He keeps count
c) He keeps chickens

*Check out **COVENANT** in your XTB Bible Dictionary.*

Did you know?

Many people who lived near the Israelites prayed to pretend gods. They **hoped** these gods would hear them and be good to them—but they could never be **sure**. They were often disappointed. But it was <u>different</u> for the Israelites. They knew that their God (the One true God) was not only real, but <u>always</u> did what He said He would do. They could **trust** Him.

You can trust God too! He will always do what He says, and never let you down.

PRAY There is **no one** like God! Use the words you wrote at the beginning of this page to praise and thank Him.

DAY 29 PHONE A FRIEND

Think of a famous person you'd love to talk to. A footballer? A pop star? Someone from the royal family? Write their name here:

Now imagine that they phone you up! How would you feel?

Today's Bible verses are about talking to someone fabulous and famous—but it's not a pop or sports star!

Read the next part of Solomon's prayer...

READ
1 Kings 8v25-30

Yesterday we saw that there is <u>no one</u> like God. What else does Solomon say about God? (v27)

a) The temple isn't fantastic enough to be God's house.

b) The temple isn't good enough, but the earth is.

c) Nothing is good enough or great enough for God!

Wow! God is awesome!!!
But what does our amazing God do when we pray? (v30)

He h_____ us!

Have you ever stopped to think how fantastic that is???
God is the all-powerful Creator of our universe—but we can talk to Him anywhere, anytime about anything. And He hears us. That's loads better than a phone chat with David Beckham!

Look up **PRAYER** in your XTB Bible Dictionary. You will see that some words are missing. Fill in the gaps using these words:

God   anywhere   anytime   anything

PRAY

Thank God that you can talk to Him anywhere, anytime about anything. Tell Him how that makes you feel.

DAY 30 HEAR OUR PRAYERS

In the second half of Solomon's prayer, he lists lots of stuff that might happen to the Israelites—and asks God to hear their prayers at all of those times. *Take the first letter of each pic to see what they were.*

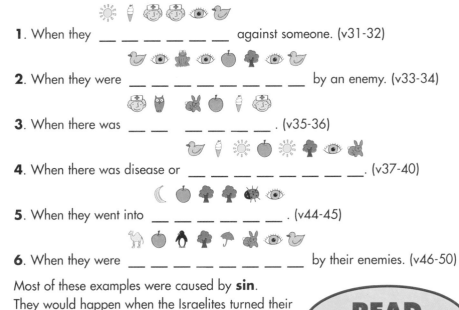

1. When they ___ ___ ___ ___ ___ ___ against someone. (v31-32)

2. When they were ___ ___ ___ ___ ___ ___ ___ ___ by an enemy. (v33-34)

3. When there was ___ ___ ___ ___ ___ ___. (v35-36)

4. When there was disease or ___ ___ ___ ___ ___ ___ ___. (v37-40)

5. When they went into ___ ___ ___ ___ ___. (v44-45)

6. When they were ___ ___ ___ ___ ___ ___ ___ by their enemies. (v46-50)

Most of these examples were caused by **sin**. They would happen when the Israelites turned their backs on God and did what <u>they</u> wanted instead. Even 'No rain' happened because of their sin...

READ
1 Kings 8v35-36

Solomon asked God to hear His people's prayers, even when their problems had been caused by their own sin!

THINK SPOT When we sin, it makes God sad and angry. But it needn't stop us from praying! If we tell God we are sorry, and ask Him to help us, He will always hear us.

THINK + PRAY We all let God down sometimes—but it doesn't mean we can't pray to Him! Think carefully about the last few days. What do you need to say sorry to God for? Tell Him you are sorry, and ask Him to help you change. Then thank Him that you are always able to pray to Him, even when you've let Him down.

DAY 31 ALL PEOPLES ON EARTH

1 Kings 8v41-43

Unjumble the letters to find the names of eight countries.

DANACA
_____

FANLIND
_____

STANDCOL
_____

CHAIN
_____

DANII
_____

GRAINIE
_____

ZILBRA
_____

AILARTSUA
_____

Solomon had just built the <u>Jewish</u> temple. But he included <u>non-Jews</u> in his prayer too, and asked God to hear them when they prayed.

> Who did Solomon want to know about God? (v43)
> **a)** Just the Israelites
> **b)** A few people from other countries too
> **c)** Everyone in the whole world

Today, there are Christians living in every part of the world! They come from <u>different countries</u>, and speak <u>different languages</u>, but they all love and obey the <u>same God</u>.

Did you notice yesterday that we skipped a bit of Solomon's prayer? The bit we missed is about us!!!

READ
1 Kings 8v41-43

THINK + PRAY

Which country do <u>you</u> live in?
_____

Mark it with an **X** *on the map.* Thank God that the great message about Him is taught in <u>your</u> country too. And thank Him that you can always pray to Him—even if you spend your hols in Greenland!!

Answers: Canada, Scotland, Finland, China, Brazil, Nigeria, India, Australia

DAY 32 GOD IS OUR KING

xtb 1 Kings 8v54-61

After Solomon finished his prayer, he stood up and blessed the Israelites.

READ
1 Kings 8v54-61

Praise the **LORD**, who has given His people **peace** as He promised. He has kept **all** the good **promises** He made through Moses.
May God be **with** us; may He never leave us or **abandon** us. May He make us **obedient** to **Him**. May all the **people** of the **earth** know that the LORD is **God** and there is **no** other.

Did you know?

Moses lived 300 years before Solomon. But in all that time, God had never broken a promise! (v56)

Fit the blue words into the puzzle.

What do the **yellow boxes** spell? ✏

___ ___ ___   ___ ___ ___   ___ ___ ___ ___

'The LORD is God—and there is no other.' (v60) This means that God is the **King** of everything.

What did Solomon say the Israelites must do? (v61)
a) Obey God's commands
b) Ignore God's commands
c) Change God's commands

PRAY

Is God the King of your life? **If He is**, you need to obey His commands too. Ask Him to help you do this. **If you're not sure**, flick back to 'Judge and Rescuer' after Day 13.

Think of three reasons for having a party:

1. _____

2. _____

3. _____

Now crack the code to see why Solomon and co. had a party.

___ ___ ___ ___ ___ ___ ___ ___ ___ ___ ___ ___ ___ ___

___ ___ ___ ___ ___ ___

Their celebrations lasted at least a week! *Break the rest of the code to see what they did.*

___ ___ ___ ___ ___ ___ ___ ___ of Shelters
(also called the Feast of Tabernacles)

___ ___ ___ ___ ___ ___ ___ ___ ___ ___ ___

Arrow Code

⇧ = A
⇨ = C
⇘ = D
⇩ = E
⇗ = F
⇦ = G
⇖ = H
↑ = I
↘ = L
↓ = M
← = O
◁ = R
▷ = S
◁ = T
▷ = V
◁ = W

  Check out **Festival of Shelters** *and* **Sacrifices** *in your XTB Bible Dictionary.*

Now read about their celebrations in 1 Kings.

READ
1 Kings 8v62-66

The people went home happy after their celebrations. Why were they so happy? (v66)

_____

PRAY — ***Think*** of some ways that God has been good to *you*. (Choose at least three.) Now ***thank God*** for His goodness. Maybe you could have a party to celebrate!

DAY 34 OBEY OR DISOBEY...

xtb 1 Kings 9v1-9

God had a message for Solomon. As you read it, look out for what will happen if Solomon <u>obeys</u> God, and what will happen if he <u>doesn't</u>...

READ
1 Kings 9v1-9

Circle the correct answers.

I have heard your **prayer/song/speech**. If you serve me as your **brother/father/uncle** David did, and **obey/disobey/ignore** my laws, then I will allow your family to rule **Egypt/Israel/England** for ever. But if you turn away from me, if you **displease/disappear/disobey** me and serve other **gods/masters/people**, then I will remove Israel from the **house/game/land** and I will abandon this **tent/temperature/temple**.

Answers: prayer, father, obey, Israel, disobey, gods, land, temple

God has made things very clear to Solomon. If he serves God like his father David did, then God will <u>bless</u> him and his people. But if he turns away from God, he will be <u>punished</u>.

THINK SPOT

What do you think Solomon will do?
Will he serve God, or turn away from Him?

We'll find out what Solomon does in the next few days.

THINK + PRAY

What about <u>you</u>? Do you want to love and serve God with every part of your life? Or are you in danger of making other things more important than God? Think carefully—and then talk to God about your answers.

DAY 35 WISDOM AND WEALTH

Ben's brilliant on the guitar!

He tells great jokes too! I wish I was like him...

Think about the leaders at your church or Christian group. What are they specially good at?

Flashback

When Solomon first became king, God offered to give him anything he asked for. Do you remember what Solomon wanted?

W_____

If you're not sure, check Day 17.

God gave Solomon **wisdom**—and great **wealth** too. In today's verses, someone came to see these for herself.

READ
1 Kings 10v1-9

Who came to see Solomon? (v1)

The Q_____ of S_____

She asked Solomon loads of difficult questions. How many did he answer? (v3)

None / Some / All

The Queen of Sheba was **amazed** at all she saw and heard. What did she say? (v9)

P_____
the L_____
your G_____.

The Queen of Sheba was <u>right</u> to praise God. **He** was the One who gave such wisdom and wealth to Solomon.

PRAY

Look again at the list you wrote at the start of the page. It is **God** who has given these gifts to your leaders. Praise and thank Him for them now.

DAY 36 GREATER THAN SOLOMON

 **xtb** Matthew 12v42

The Queen of Sheba travelled 1000 miles to listen to Solomon's wisdom. She was very impressed.

The rest of **1 Kings 10** lists the amazing riches of Solomon's kingdom. She was impressed by that too—almost everything was made of *gold!*

But, wise and wealthy though Solomon was, he was just a man. We're going to jump into the New Testament today to meet someone far more impressive than Solomon...

READ
Matthew 12v42

The Queen of Sheba is called the Queen of the South by Jesus. What did she travel a huge distance to do? (v42)

> To l_____
>
> to Solomon's
>
> w_____

What did Jesus say about that? (v42)

> Someone
>
> g_____
>
> than Solomon is here.

Jesus was talking about Himself! *Use these words to fill in the gaps.*

great   greater   wise   wiser   king   King

• Solomon was **w**_____, but Jesus is **w**_____.

• Solomon was **g**_____, but Jesus is **g**_____.

• Solomon was **k**_____ of Israel, but Jesus is **K**_____ of the world!

THINK + PRAY

The Queen of Sheba travelled a long way to listen to Solomon. But it's far better (and more important) to listen to King Jesus! Ask Him to help you listen to what He says in the Bible, and to obey His words.

DAY 37 LED ASTRAY...

*Take the <u>first letter</u> of each pic to see **two commands** God gave His people.*

Do not _ _ _ _ _ _ people from _ _ _ _ _ _ nations, because they will lead you to worship other gods.
Deuteronomy 7v3-4

The king is not to have _ _ _ _ _ _ _ _ _ because this would make him turn away from the LORD.
Deuteronomy 17v17

Now read today's verses to see what **Solomon** did.

READ
1 Kings 11v1-3

Did Solomon have many wives? (v3)   **Yes / No**

How many??? (v3)

Did Solomon marry women from other nations? (v1) **Yes / No**

God had given <u>good</u> rules, so that His people wouldn't turn away from Him. But Solomon <u>broke</u> God's rules...

READ
1 Kings 11v4-6

When did Solomon's wives turn his heart away from God? (v4)
  a) At once
  b) As he grew old
  c) Never

It didn't happen straight away. But <u>slowly</u> Solomon changed, so that God wasn't 'No.1' in his life any more.

THINK + PRAY

Is God **No.1** in your life? What things or people might slowly become more important to you than loving and serving God? Ask God to help you not to slip away from Him as Solomon did.

DAY 38 SOLOMON LOVED...

Solomon's story started with these words:

Solomon loved the  _ _ _ _
1 Kings 3v3

But it ends with very different words:

Solomon loved many foreign
_ _ _ _ _ . 1 Kings 11v1

God wasn't **No.1** in Solomon's heart any more. And as a result, Solomon turned to other gods (the pretend gods his wives believed in).

Solomon had built a magnificent temple for the One True God. But now he built places of worship for these pretend gods!

READ
1 Kings 11v7-13

_ _ _ _ _ _ _ _ _ _ _

How did God feel about Solomon? (v9)

God was a_____

On Day 34 we read God's words to Solomon. He warned Solomon that he would be punished if he turned away from God.

God's punishment was to take the kingdom away from Solomon, and make someone else king instead.

_ _ _ _ _

Grace is God's huge kindness to people who don't deserve it. God was right to punish Solomon, but He also showed him grace. The punishment would be delayed until after Solomon's death, and Solomon's son would still rule over part of the kingdom (v13).

Punishment and Grace

All sin must be **punished**. That includes all the times when you and I let God down by doing what we want instead of what He wants.

But God showed His amazing **grace** to us by sending His own Son Jesus to take the punishment we deserve.

We'll think about this more on Day 40.

PRAY

Say sorry to God for the times you have let Him down. Thank Him for sending Jesus to take your punishment, so that you can be forgiven.

DAY 39 GOD KEEPS HIS WORD

Flashback One

God had promised David that his son would become ▨ ● ▨ ▥ __ __ __ __
after him. (*That promise is in 2 Samuel 7v12-13.*)
God kept His word—and Solomon became king after David.

Flashback Two

God also told David that when his son did <u>wrong</u>, God would use

▢ ▨ ▨ ● ▪ ▢

other men to __ __ __ __ __ __ him.
(*That promise is in 2 Samuel 7v14.*)
God kept His word—and used three men to punish Solomon.

Read the verses to discover their names.

READ 1 Kings 11v14 ➝ H_____ the Edomite.

READ 1 Kings 11v23 ➝ R_____ son of Eliada.

READ 1 Kings 11v26 ➝ J_____ son of Nebat.

Flag Code

▬ = **E**
▥ = **G**
▢ = **H**
● = **I**
▤ = **J**
▨ = **K**
▨ = **N**
▢ = **P**
▪ = **S**
▨ = **U**

God used **Hadad**, **Rezon** and **Jeroboam** to punish Solomon—just as He said He would.

THINK SPOT

God <u>always</u> keeps His word. That means He always gives the good things He has promised. It also means that He always punishes when He says He will.

THINK + PRAY

God's words always come true. That means everything you read in the Bible is true. How does that make you feel? Talk to God about it.

xtb 1 Kings 11v41-43

READ
1 Kings 11v41-43

How long did Solomon rule as king for? (v42)

_____ **years**

Who became king after him? (v43)

R_____

In the end, Solomon's son Rehoboam was only king of a <u>bit</u> of Israel.

Just as God had said!

Solomon had started out really well:
- He **loved** God like his father David had done. (Day 16)
- He asked God for **wisdom** to help him rule. (Day 17)
- He built the **temple** for God. (Day 23)

But Solomon turned away from God:
- He let God down.
- He let his people down too.

> God's people needed a king who would love God totally. They needed a king who would love <u>them</u> too, and show them how to live for God.

1000 years after Solomon, this kind of king was born. _Use yesterday's code to see his name._

_ _ _ _ _

1. King Jesus lived a **perfect** life. He never let God down.
2. King Jesus **loves** His people—so much that He died for them!
3. King Jesus came back to life, and **rules today** as King of the world.
4. One day, King Jesus will **come back** to our world. And He will welcome His forgiven friends into His wonderful kingdom for ever.

THINK + PRAY

Are **you** one of Jesus' forgiven friends, looking forward to Him coming back again? _If you're not sure_, <u>read</u> 'Am I a Christian?' just before Day 14. _If you are sure_, <u>thank</u> King Jesus now for the four things listed above.

DAY 41 JUMP BACK TO JOHN

Welcome back to John's book about Jesus.
Do you remember why John wrote his book?
Go forward one letter to fill in the missing words.
(A=B, B=C, C=D etc)

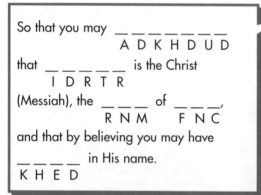

So that you may _ _ _ _ _ _ _ _
        A D K H D U D

that _ _ _ _ _ is the Christ
   I D R T R

(Messiah), the _ _ _ of _ _ _,
     R N M   F N C

and that by believing you may have

_ _ _ _ in His name.
K H E D

(You can find the answer in **John 20 v 31**)

John wants us to believe that Jesus is
the Christ/Messiah—God's chosen King.

In his book, John tells us loads of amazing things that Jesus did and said.

They are all *signposts* pointing to who Jesus is. They help us understand more about Jesus.

PRAY

Thank God that you can read all about Jesus in John's book. Ask God to help you learn loads about Jesus and to understand who He really is.

Turn to the next page now!

READ John 6v1-4

Why did lots of people follow Jesus? (Fill in the missing word.)

Because they saw the m_____ he had performed (v2).

People wanted to see Jesus do more miracles. But John tells us they are **signs** that show us who Jesus is.

READ John 6v5-9

Where can we **b_____** enough bread for all these **p_____**?

Lots and lots of money couldn't buy enough **b_____**.

This boy has 5 small **l_____** and 2 small **f_____**. But it will never feed all these people!

The disciples didn't understand that Jesus was God's Son and could easily feed thousands of people.

 *Check out '**disciple**' in your XTB Bible Dictionary.*

READ John 6v10-11

That's amazing! Jesus fed thousands of people with just 5 loaves of bread and 2 small fish! This was a **sign** that Jesus was **God's Son**. Only God's Son could do such amazing things.

PRAY Only Jesus can give everything we need. That means you need Him! Pray about this. (*More about this on Day 45.*)

DAY 42 WHO IS JESUS?

Jesus has just fed thousands of people with a tiny picnic! It was a **signpost** pointing to the fact that Jesus is **God's Son**.

READ
John 6v12-13

How many baskets did the disciples fill with scraps?

Only **JESUS** could do a miracle like that!

READ
John 6v14-15

Flag	= Letter
▬	= E
⫴⫴⫴	= G
▯	= H
⚫	= I
▐	= K
▦	= N
◨	= O
⬜	= P
✚	= R
▮	= T

Who did the people think Jesus was? Use the **flag code**.

_ _ _ _ _ _ _ _ _

The people thought that Jesus was God's messenger that Moses had talked about. They were **right!**

Read about 'the Prophet' in your XTB Bible Dictionary.

But what did they want Jesus to become (v15)?

_ _ _ _ _ _ _ _ _ _ _ _

They thought Jesus had come to kick the Romans out of their country and take over as king. But they were **wrong!**

Jesus had come to be King. But King of their lives, not king of their country! And He had come to rescue them. But to rescue them from <u>sin</u>, not from the <u>Romans</u>! Do you want to know how Jesus can rescue us from sin? Then turn to **Judge and Rescuer** after Day 13.

THINK + PRAY Is Jesus the King in charge of your life? Ask God to help you to live your life for Jesus.

DAY 43 WALKING ON WHAT? ER?

What are you scared of?
Circle the things that frighten you!

the dark

In today's story, the disciples are in a boat on a dark, stormy night. But it's not the storm they're scared of—it's **Jesus!**

READ
John 6v16-21

When they saw Jesus walking on the lake they were terrified! But what did Jesus say to them (v20)? *Cross out all the **X**s to find out.*

XXXXDXXOXXXNXXOXXXTXXXB
XXXEXXAXXXFXXRXXAXXIXXDXXX

D_____

The disciples saw something really scary—someone with superhuman power! What would He do to them?? **But** when they realised it was their great Friend Jesus they felt O.K.

THINK SPOT

This was another sign that Jesus is God's King. He's totally powerful. If you don't know Him, you should be scared. But if Jesus is your King, He loves you. You don't need to be afraid of Him or anything else!

READ
John 6v22-24

The crowd couldn't work out how Jesus had crossed the lake without a boat! But we know how! And we also know that Jesus is the Christ—God's chosen King.

PRAY
Thank God that Jesus is the King. Ask Him to be yours too—so you don't need to be afraid of anything!

DAY 44 ONE WAY ONLY

Jesus was really popular! Crowds of people followed Him everywhere. They'd heard all about how He fed thousands of people with only five loaves and two fish. They were hoping He'd give them food too.

READ
John 6v25-27

What did Jesus say they should want more than bread? Take the **first letter** of each picture to find out.

_ _ _ _ _ _ _   _ _ _ _

That means living for ever with God in heaven!

Who could give them eternal life (v27)?

_ _ _ _ _   _ _ _ _ _ _ _

That means Jesus! And Jesus said that God was really pleased with Him.

 John 6v25-29

READ
John 6v28-29

How do we get eternal life (v29)?

_ _ _ _ _ _ _ _ _ _ _ _ _ _ _ _

_ _ _ _ _ _ _ _ _ _ _ _ _ _

Lots of people think that doing good deeds is enough to get them to heaven.
But Jesus says there's nothing **we** can **do** to get us into heaven. Good deeds aren't enough. We must **believe in Jesus.** Only He can give us eternal life.

PRAY

Ask God to help you believe and trust in **Jesus**. Forget about good deeds—make sure you get eternal life!

DAY 45 BREAD FROM HEAVEN

Jesus told the crowd that He could give them everlasting life in heaven! But they wouldn't believe Him...

READ
John 6v30-33

Give us a **sign** to prove what you're saying. Moses gave us bread from heaven. Can **you** do that?

*Use words from the **word pool** to complete what Jesus said to them.*

WORD POOL
**Moses   bread   He
God   heaven   world
life   thirsty   hungry**

It is **G**_____ who gives you **b**_____ from heaven, not **M**_____. The bread that God gives is **H**_____ who comes down from **h**_____ and gives life to the **w**_____.

God has given us something much better than bread—He's given us His Son **Jesus**!

READ
John 6v34-35

I am the bread of **l**_____. Whoever comes to me will never go **h**_____ or **t**_____.

Jesus means that if we trust in Him, He will give us everything we really need. He will forgive our sins! And give us everlasting life in heaven!

Have you trusted Jesus for those things? Do you really believe that He can give them to you?

THINK SPOT

PRAY Thank God for giving us the best gift ever—Jesus!

DAY 46 NEVER LET GO!

 Check out *'eternal life'* in your XTB Dictionary

 John 6v36-40

Jesus has been telling the crowds amazing things about Himself.

READ
John 6v40

Use the **shape code** to unscramble what Jesus said.

Everyone who trusts Jesus will have

_____ _____

That's brilliant! Anyone can live for ever in heaven! When Jesus returns to earth, everyone who has trusted Him will be raised back to life, to live with Him for ever! (Want to know how you can trust Jesus? Turn to 'Judge and Rescuer' after Day 13.)

READ
John 6v36-39

Jesus has great news for everyone who trusts Him. That means all **Christians**.

SHAPE CODE

A = ■
E = ■
F = ■
I = ●
L = ●
N = ●
O = ●
R = ◆
T = ◆
U = ◆
W = ◆
Y = ★

Whoever comes to me

_____ _____ ____ _____

_____ _____

Now there's no reason to miss out on eternal life. **Jesus will never turn you away or lose you.** Except... you must <u>come</u> to Him—that means trust and obey Him. So, is that how you live?

REALLY COOL!

PRAY

"Dear God, thank you for sending Jesus. Thank you that He never turns away anyone who trusts in Him."

Do you like bread? **YES / NO**

READ
John 6v41-48

The people couldn't believe that this ordinary looking man could give them eternal life. But they didn't realise that **GOD** had sent Jesus to them.

Now fill in the missing **E**s to reveal what Jesus said in verse 47.

H__ who b__li__v__s has __v__rlasting lif__

Jesus makes it possible for us to live for ever. We just have to believe Him and trust Him. And that means living His way too.

READ
John 6v49-51

What else did Jesus say?

This br__ad is my fl__sh (body), that I will giv__ for th__ lif__ of th__ world.

Jesus had to **die** so that we can have eternal life. We deserve to die for all the wrong things we've done. But Jesus took the punishment in our place. He **died** so that we can **live** for ever!

For the free booklet **Why did Jesus die?** write to XTB, 37 Elm Road, New Malden, Surrey, KT3 3HB. Or email alison@thegoodbook.co.uk

PRAY Is there anything you want to thank Jesus for? Anything you want to tell Him?

DAY 48 FOOD FOR THOUGHT

 John 6v52-59

Why do we eat food? (Tick some.)

- because it tastes great ☐
- to keep mum happy ☐
- to live / to keep us alive ☐

All of those answers are true, but the most important reason is that we eat food to **live**.

Jesus said He was the **bread of life**. The crowd got confused and thought He meant they should actually eat Him!

READ
John 6v52-59

This must be really important if Jesus keeps repeating it! But He doesn't mean that people have to eat Him!

Go forward one letter to work out what Jesus means (**A=B, B=C, C=D, Z=A etc**).

X	N	T		B	Z	M

N	M	K	X		G	Z	U	D

D	S	D	Q	M	Z	K

K	H	E	D		A	X

L	X		C	D	Z	S	G

Jesus gave up His own life so that we can have **eternal life**. Trusting in Jesus is a bit like eating. We must eat to live, and we must trust Jesus for eternal life.

 THINK SPOT

It's crazy to give up food. No food = death! Similarly, it's crazy to give up trusting Jesus. No Jesus = no eternal life. Nothing's more important!

PRAY

Ask God to help you fully trust in Jesus. To truly believe that Jesus' death makes it possible for you to have eternal life.

Jesus claimed to be the **bread of life**—the only way to eternal life in heaven. Many of Jesus' followers wouldn't believe Him. (*In today's Bible verses, **disciples** means <u>all</u> of Jesus' followers, not just the twelve disciples*).

READ
John 6v60-62

*Check out '**disciple**' and '**Holy Spirit**' in your XTB Dictionary.*

These people refused to believe Jesus. But Jesus knew that these hangers-on wouldn't stick by Him when He was killed on the cross and went back to heaven.

READ
John 6v63

Complete what Jesus said by reading the **backwards** words.

THE S_____ GIVES L_____.
     TIRIPS   EFIL

F_____ COUNTS FOR N_____.
  HSELF   GNIHTON

These people were only interested in earthly things—food, money, living a good life. They weren't really interested in **SPIRITUAL** things—godly things. That's why they wouldn't believe Jesus. But only **JESUS** could give them eternal life in heaven!

READ
John 6v64-66

What did many of Jesus' followers do (v66)?

T_____ B_____
DENRUT   KCAB

They refused to believe Him and live His way. Do you know anyone who won't have anything to do with Jesus? _____

_____

PRAY

Ask God to turn their lives around, so that they come to love Jesus and live His way. And yours, if you're only into earthly things!

DAY 50 THE CHOICE IS YOURS

In his book about Jesus, John has given us loads of **SIGNPOSTS** to help us believe that Jesus is **the Christ —God's chosen King.** Now we've seen the evidence, we have a choice...

Believe Jesus, live for Him and have eternal life in heaven.

or

Don't believe Jesus, turn away from Him and live your own way.

Jesus' twelve disciples had that same choice...

READ
John 6v67-71

What did Simon Peter say to Jesus? *Take the first letter of each pic to find out.*

You have the words of

_ _ _ _ _ _ _ _ _ _

Peter knew that trusting Jesus was the only way to eternal life in heaven.

We believe that you are the

_ _ _ _ _ _ _ _ _ _ _ _

Peter believed that Jesus had been sent by God.

THINK + PRAY

Do you believe those things? Do you trust Jesus to give you eternal life? Or will you turn away like Judas did (v71)?

Tell God how you honestly feel. And ask Him to help you to really trust Jesus and live His way.

KING AND PROPHET

Welcome back to the book of 1 Kings!

Last time, we read about King Solomon. Now we're jumping ahead a few chapters to meet a new king—but first, **crack the code** to see what happened after Solomon's death.

- The Israelites were split into __ __ __ kingdoms.

- The northern kingdom was called __ __ __ __ __ __.

- The southern kingdom was called __ __ __ __ __.

We're going to read about the northern kingdom of **Israel**. They'd had a whole bunch of bad kings, but their new king was the worst of all!

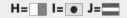

A=◧ B=◩ D=▬ E=▭

H=◪ I=● J=▭

L=◰ O=◩ R=◫ S=■

T=▯ U=◱ W=□

His name was __ __ __ __

READ
1 Kings 16v29-30

How bad was Ahab? (v30)

a) He only sinned a little bit.

b) He sinned nearly as much as the kings before him.

c) He sinned far more than any king before him.

Ahab was the most evil king of Israel. He even built a temple for the pretend god Baal, and then served Baal instead of God!!! (v31-33)

But God cared for His people, the Israelites.
So God sent them one of His prophets (God's messengers).

His name was __ __ __ __ __ __.

READ
1 Kings 17v1-6

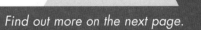

Find out more on the next page.

Fill in the gaps from v1.

> I serve the **L**_____, the God of Israel. I tell you that there will be no **d**_____ or **r**_____ in the next few **y**_____ unless I say so.

years   LORD   rain   dew

Elijah was in danger from King Ahab. So God told him to hide out for a while. God made sure that Elijah had the food and water he needed.

Where did the water come from? (v4)   **A b**_____

Where did the food come from? (v6)

It was brought by r_____!

Did you know?

King Ahab worshipped Baal, who was supposed to be the god of rain and storms. But Elijah reminded Ahab that **God** is the real God of Israel. By stopping the rain, God showed that He is in charge, and that Baal was fake and powerless.

PRAY

God was going to use Elijah to teach King Ahab and the Israelites some very important things. Ask God to help you to learn more about Him too as you read about Elijah in 1 Kings.

Elijah was hiding from Ahab. God had stopped the rain, so Elijah drank water from a brook. And his food was brought by ravens! But then the brook dried up...

God spoke to Elijah.

Go to the town of Zarephath near Sidon and stay there.

I have commanded a widow who lives there to feed you.

So Elijah went to Zarephath, and found the widow gathering sticks.

Please bring me a drink of water.

And please bring me some bread.

As surely as the Lord your God lives, I tell you the truth.

I have no bread.

I have only a handful of flour in a jar and a little olive oil in a jug.

I have come here to gather some wood. I will take it home and cook our last meal.

My son and I will eat it – and then die from hunger.

But Elijah had good news for her...

Don't be afraid!

Why shouldn't she be afraid?
Read the verses to find out.

READ
1 Kings 17v13-16

Taken from 1 Kings 17v7-13

What was God's message to the widow? (v14)

The jar of **f_____** will not be used up, and the jug of **o_____** will not run dry until the day the LORD gives **r_____** on the land.

rain
oil
flour

Did God's words come true? (v16)   **Yes / No**

THINK + PRAY

Do you think it was easy for that widow to trust God? Why/why not?

Do *you* find it easy to trust God? Talk to Him about your answer.

The story so far...

- <u>King</u> Ahab served Baal instead of <u>God</u>
- So God stopped the <u>rain</u>!
- God's prophet <u>Elijah</u> hid by a brook
- God sent <u>ravens</u> to feed him!
- Then Elijah went to stay with a <u>widow</u>
- God gave her never-ending <u>flour</u> & oil!

Fit the **underlined words** into the puzzle.

		I					
		O	U				
		O					
	I		O				
	E		I		A		
	A	I					
A		E					

— — — — — — —

All through the story of Elijah, there's a kind of competition between Baal and God. And <u>every</u> time: **GOD WINS!!!**

Elijah stayed with a widow who lived near Sidon, outside Israel. People there believed in Baal. But it was **God** who gave the widow never-ending food—not Baal! **GOD WINS!!!**

But then her son became ill...

READ
1 Kings 17v17-24

What happened to the widow's son? (v17)

He _____

Elijah carried the dead boy up to his room, and cried out to God for help. What was his prayer? (v21)

> O LORD my God

Did God bring the boy back to life? (v22) **Yes / No**

How do you think his mum felt?

What did she say? (v24)

truth   know   God   word

> Now I **k**_____ that you are a man of **G**_____ and that the **w**_____ of the Lord from your mouth is **t**_____.

She was right! God's words are <u>always</u> true.

PRAY Thank God that His words in the Bible are both true and powerful.

DAY 54 TWO WAYS TO SERVE

King Ahab and the Israelites had been worshipping Baal instead of God. So God punished them by sending no rain for three whole years!!!

READ
1 Kings 18v1

What was God going to do? (v1)

> Send r_____

So God told Elijah to go and see Ahab.

Did you know?

Evil King Ahab had been searching for Elijah for three years, but God had kept him safely hidden. Ahab's wife, Jezebel, <u>hated</u> the followers of God. She had **killed** many of the prophets (God's messengers).

Not all of Ahab's men were enemies of God. One of them had been helping God's prophets...

READ
1 Kings 18v2-8

What had Obadiah done? (v4)
   a) Killed 100 prophets
   b) Rescued 100 prophets
   c) Rescued 100 porcupines

What a brave thing to do! Obadiah was working for King Ahab, yet he secretly went against the king and hid 100 of God's prophets in caves!

Ahab had sent Obadiah to look for grass for the animals. But who did Obadiah find instead? (v7)

> ✏️ _____

Obadiah was worried that Elijah would hide again, but he agreed to tell Ahab that Elijah was here (v9-15).
Tomorrow we'll see what happens when Ahab and Elijah meet up...

THINK+ PRAY

Elijah was God's messenger and boldly told people what God had to say.

Obadiah served God secretly and bravely saved 100 prophets.

Elijah and Obadiah served God in different ways. Ask God to show you how <u>you</u> can serve Him best.

DAY 55 CARMEL CONTEST

xtb 1 Kings 18v16-21

There's an important question running through chapter 18 of 1 Kings. *Crack the code to see what it is.*

◁ ⇘ ← ⬆ ▷ ◁ ⇘ ⬇ ▽ ⬇ ⬆ ⬊ ⇦ ← ⇘

_ _ _ _ _ _ _ _ _ _ _ _ _ _ _ ?

The Bible shows us again and again that **God** is the One true God. But Ahab and the Israelites have been worshipping **Baal** instead! So now it's crunch time—a contest between Baal and God, at the top of Mount Carmel...

READ
1 Kings 18v16-18

What did Ahab call Elijah? (v17)

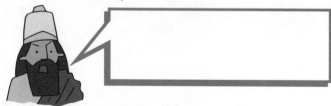

But it wasn't Elijah who'd made trouble for Israel—it was Ahab! He'd led the people to worship <u>Baal</u> instead of <u>God</u>.

⇧ = A
⇘ = D
⬇ = E
⬀ = F
⇦ = G
⇘ = H
⬆ = I
⬊ = L
⬇ = M
← = O
▽ = R
▷ = S
◁ = T
◁ = W

Elijah told Ahab to bring all of the Israelites to the top of Mount Carmel. He was to bring the 450 prophets of Baal too.

READ
1 Kings 18v19-21

What did Elijah tell the people? (v21)

If the LORD is God, ⬀ ← ⬊ ⬊ ← ◁ ⇘ ⬆ ⬇ _ _ _ _ _ _ _ _ _

But if Baal is God, ⬀ ← ⬊ ⬊ ← ◁ ⇘ ⬆ ⬇ _ _ _ _ _ _ _ _ _

More about the contest tomorrow...

PRAY

Like these people, we must choose what to do. Believing in God means following Him—doing what He wants. Do you follow God like that? If you follow what <u>you</u> or others want, you <u>don't</u> believe the LORD is God. Ask Him to help you to do what He wants in every part of your life.

DAY 56   BAAL FAILS

It's time for the Carmel contest. Elijah has set a test for both Baal and God. Two stone altars are built, with wood for a fire and a sacrifice (gift) of meat on top. One altar is for Baal, and one for God. *Spot eight differences between them.*

Baal's altar

God's altar

Elijah told the prophets of Baal that they could go first...

READ
1 Kings 18v22-26

What did Elijah say to the people? (v24)

| The god who answers by **fire**—he is _____. |

Was there an answer from Baal? (v26)   **Yes / No**

When there was no answer, Elijah made fun of the prophets of Baal. He told them to shout louder!

READ
1 Kings 18v27-29

Was there an answer from Baal this time? (v29)   **Yes / No**

Did you know?

Baal can rhyme with 'fail'—which is cool, 'cos Baal fails!!

*Write '**No answer**' across the picture of Baal's altar.*

THINK + PRAY

Elijah suggested that Baal wasn't answering because he was asleep! (v27) But the One true God _isn't_ like that. Psalm 121 reminded the Israelites that God was their protector, who 'never dozes or sleeps' (Psalm 121v4). That's true today too. Thank God that He is always looking after you, and never asleep, no matter what time of day (or night!) it is.

DAY 57 GOD WINS

The Carmel contest is under way. Two altars have been built. Whoever can set the sacrifice on fire is the true God.

Yesterday we saw how Baal failed miserably. Of course he did; he's a fake god who doesn't exist!!!

Baal's altar

The prophets of Baal had spent all day shouting, dancing and cutting themselves. But there was **no answer** to their cries.

Now it was Elijah's turn...

READ
1 Kings 18v30-35

Elijah rebuilt God's altar, using twelve stones for the twelve Israelite tribes. He was reminding the Israelites that **God was their God**, and they were <u>His</u> people.

What did Elijah pour over the altar? (v33)   **W**_____

How many times??? (v34) _____ **times**

Draw water dripping from the wood and meat, and filling the trench round God's altar.

The wet wood would be hard to set on fire. But **nothing is too hard for God!!!**

READ
1 Kings 18v36-39

Draw God's fire burning up the altar. It burnt the meat, the wood and even the stones!

What did the people cry out? (v39)

The LORD
_____
The LORD
_____

Draw their faces.

PRAY

God really is the One true God. Nobody and nothing can compete with Him! Spend some time praising God—and remember that nothing is too hard for Him!

DAY 58 FIRE PROOF

The question running through chapter 18 is **'Who is the real God?'**.
*Cross out all the **A**s, **B**s and **C**s in the puzzle, then follow the maze to see the answer.*

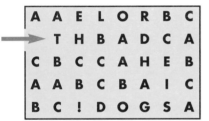

A	A	E	L	O	R	B	C
T	H	B	A	D	C	A
C	B	C	C	A	H	E	B
A	A	B	C	B	A	I	C
B	C	!	D	O	G	S	A

T _ _   _ _ _ _

_ _ _   _ _ _   _ _ _ ! (v39)

The Israelites said this when God sent fire to burn up His altar. They finally realised that **God** is the <u>real</u> God!

The prophets of Baal had led the people <u>away</u> from God, so they were rightly punished—by death. (v40)

Back in verse 1, God said He would send rain. Now the time had come. Is that rain I hear??

READ
1 Kings 18v41-46

How many times did Elijah send his servant to look towards the sea? (v43)

_____ **times**

What did the servant see at last? (v44)
a) A cloud as small as a man's foot
b) A cloud as small as a man's hand
c) A cloud as small as a man's left eyebrow

As Ahab set off for home, the rain poured down—**just as God had promised**. And Elijah ran in front of Ahab's chariot all the way!

Think back over the story of the Carmel contest, and choose some words to describe God.

THINK + PRAY

Now use those words to praise and thank God.

 **Circle Code**

 1 Kings 19v1-8

    _ _ _ _ _ ?

- **God** had won the Carmel contest
- The people had seen that **God** is the real God—not Baal
- **God** had kept His promise to send rain—bucketloads of it!

Did that mean everyone in Israel was happy??? Oh no!

 _ _ _ _ !

Queen Jezebel (Ahab's wife) was a follower of Baal. When she heard what happened on Mount Carmel—and that the 450 prophets of Baal had been killed—she was furious...

READ
1 Kings 19v1-3

Jezebel was out to **kill** Elijah! What did Elijah do? (v3)
  a) Ran to see Jezebel
  b) Ran for his life
  c) Ran for a bus

We don't know for sure why Elijah ran away. Maybe he had stopped trusting God. Maybe he was exhausted after the contest on Mount Carmel, and couldn't face another fight.

But we do know how he felt later...

READ
1 Kings 19v4

● ● ● _ _ _

It was too much for Elijah —he just wanted to die!

Elijah felt **awful**—but God sent him some help...

READ
1 Kings 19v5-8

What did the angel say to Elijah? (v5)

The food gave Elijah the strength he needed for his l-o-n-g journey. *Tomorrow we'll see what happened when he got there.*

PRAY

Elijah felt awful, but God took care of Him. No matter how **bad** things are, or how **sad** you feel, you can always turn to God. Talk to Him now.

If you feel bad or sad, try to find an older Christian to talk to

Sit very quietly for a minute. What can you hear?

Elijah had run away from Jezebel, who wanted to kill him. God had kept Elijah alive, and now he was hiding in a cave.

What do you think Elijah could hear?

God had a question for Elijah...

READ
1 Kings 19v9-10

What was God's question? (v9)

Elijah told God how the Israelites were breaking His covenant laws. Elijah felt like he was the only godly person left.

 *Check out **Covenant** in your XTB Bible Dictionary*

Then God told Elijah to leave the cave...

READ
1 Kings 19v11-14

Unjumble the letters to see what Elijah heard and saw.

DIWN   W_____
THEEARQUAK E_____
RIFE   F_____
WERSHIP   W_____

Was God in the **wind, earthquake** and **fire**?   **Yes / No**

No—God spoke in a gentle **whisper**.

 THINK SPOT — Sometimes, God speaks to His people through <u>spectacular</u> things (like the fire on Mount Carmel). But He often speaks <u>quietly</u>, through His Word. For Elijah that meant a **voice**. For us, it means the **Bible**.

*Look up **Bible** in your Dictionary*

THINK + PRAY — When you read the Bible, do you expect God to speak to you? Every day this week, pray before you start XTB and ask God to speak to you from His Word. Thank Him now for what He's been saying to you in the past few days.

DAY 61 JUDGEMENT AND GRACE

The story so far...

- Elijah had run away from **Jezebel**, who wanted to kill him
- Elijah felt terrible, and wanted to **die**
- God sent an **angel** to give Elijah food and water
- The food strengthened **Elijah** for a **40** day walk
- Elijah arrived at Mount **Sinai** (also called **Horeb**)
- God spoke to Elijah in a gentle **whisper**

Find the <u>yellow words</u> in the wordsearch.

Some are backwards!

J	U	L	E	B	E	Z	E	J
D	G	4	0	A	N	G	E	L
E	M	E	N	S	I	N	A	I
E	L	I	J	A	H	E	I	D
B	E	R	O	H	T	G	R	A
R	E	P	S	I	H	W	C	E

God told Elijah to appoint <u>three</u> men who would punish Ahab and the Israelites for disobeying God...

READ
1 Kings 19v15-18

Who were the three men?

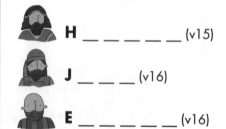

H _ _ _ _ _ (v15)

J _ _ _ (v16)

E _ _ _ _ _ _ (v16)

The leftover letters from the wordsearch spell **two words**. *Copy those letters here to see what they are.*

J _ _ _ _ _ _ _ _ _
G _ _ _ _

Judgement

Ahab and the Israelites had disobeyed God. So God would use Hazael, Jehu and Elisha to punish them.

Grace

Even though the Israelites kept disobeying God, He would keep 7000 of them safe. That's fantastic grace!

*Check out **Grace** in your XTB Bible Dictionary*

THINK + PRAY

Think of some ways that God has shown His grace to you. (*eg: answering your prayers, sending Jesus to save you from your sins...*) Thank God for these things now.

DAY 62 GOD'S CHARACTER

Yesterday we saw two sides of God's character. They seem quite different, but both have to be there—like the two sides of the same coin...

Judgement

God makes sure that sin is punished.

Grace

God's HUGE kindness to people who don't deserve it.

God brought **judgement** on the Israelites by choosing three men who would punish them for disobeying Him.

God showed His **grace** by promising that 7000 Israelites would be kept safe.

 =A   =C   =E   =G

Flag Code

 =H   =N   =O   =T

Crack the flag code to see something God says about Himself:

I the LORD do

_ _ _   _ _ _ _   _ _ _

(Malachi 3v6)

God never changes! That means He is a God of **judgement** and **grace** today as well.

THINK SPOT

We all **sin** (we all do what we want instead of what God wants). God's right **judgement** of our sin is that it must be punished. But God has also shown His **grace** to us. Do you know how? *Think carefully about your answer, and then check it by reading Jesus' words in today's verse.*

READ
John 5v24

God has shown us His grace by sending His own Son Jesus to save us!

*Find out more by reading **Judge and Rescuer** after Day 13.*

THINK + PRAY

Have you been rescued by Jesus? *(If you're not sure, read 'Am I a Christian?' again, just before Day 14).* If you are a Christian, you'll want to tell your friends about Jesus too. Ask God to help you to do that this week.

DAY 63 FAREWELL TO FARMING

xtb 1 Kings 19v19-21

God had told Elijah to appoint **Elisha**. He was to be the next <u>prophet</u> (God's messenger) after Elijah...

READ
1 Kings 19v19-21

Use the wordpool to fill in the news report.

> burned cloak Elijah Elisha
> family helper messenger oxen people
> ploughing prophet Shaphat

READ ALL ABOUT IT!

RICH FARMER THROWS IT ALL AWAY

In surprising news, **E**_____, son of wealthy farmer **S**_____, has turned his back on the **f**_____ business. Instead, he has taken the post of **h**_____ to **E**_____ the famous **p**_____. When asked why he took such a low-paying job, Elisha said, 'Elijah came up and threw his **c**_____ around me to show that one day I'll take his place as God's **m**_____'. To show he was serious about his career change, Elisha **b**_____ all the **p**_____ equipment and turned his **o**_____ into steaks for the **p**_____!

Elisha was to be Elijah's servant. That meant doing stuff like pouring water on Elijah's hands before a meal (2 Kings 3v11). Not very exciting stuff! But **God** had called Elisha to do it, so he threw himself into it straight away.

THINK + PRAY

Sometimes God wants us to serve Him in <u>little</u> things. *(Helping out at home, doing the cleaning at church, etc)* But it's still serving God and it still pleases Him! Think of some ways that you can serve God this week. Now ask Him to help you to get stuck into serving Him, even in the less exciting jobs.

DAY 64 TIME TO GO

We're going to jump into the book of **2 Kings** to finish the story of Elijah. As we join them, Elijah and Elisha are visiting lots of spots in Israel...

READ
2 Kings 2v1-6

Where did they visit?

G _ _ _ _ _ (v1)

B _ _ _ _ _ (v2)

J _ _ _ _ _ _ (v4)

J _ _ _ _ _ (v6)

*Check out **Elijah's last journey** in your XTB Bible Dictionary to see where these places were.*

READ
2 Kings 2v7-10

What happened when Elijah struck the river Jordan with his cloak? (v8)

a) The water turned to ice and they skated across.

b) The water divided and they crossed on dry land.

c) The water made his cloak wet!

Wow! God parted the river Jordan for Elijah and Elisha. Just like He parted the Red Sea so Moses and the Israelites could escape the Egyptians. (Exodus 14v21-22)

Elisha wanted to carry on Elijah's work after he was gone. He wanted to serve God as His messenger to the Israelites. *(That's what v9 means.)*

Elijah said it was up to God—but it would happen if Elisha <u>saw</u> Elijah going up to heaven. *We'll find out the answer to that tomorrow...*

THINK+PRAY

We are <u>all</u> called to serve God. The Bible tells us loads of ways to do that *(eg: telling friends about Jesus, loving other people, praying for people who are ill or who need help...)* Ask God to help you serve Him like this, and also to show you any special jobs He has just for <u>you</u> *(eg: you may be the only Christian your friend knows, so it's <u>your</u> special job to tell them about Jesus).*

DAY 65 CHARIOT OF FIRE

Yesterday's story left us with two questions:
1. How will Elijah go to heaven?
2. Will Elisha see him go?

Both are answered in today's reading...

READ
2 Kings 2v11-18

How did Elijah go to heaven? (v11)

Draw or write your answer here.

Did Elisha see him go? (v12)

Yes / No

God gave Elisha **3 signs** that he was to be God's prophet after Elijah. *Take the first letter of each pic to see them.*

1

_ _ _ _ _ _ , _

_ _ _ _ _

Elisha picked up Elijah's cloak to show that he was carrying on Elijah's work as prophet (v13).

2

_ _ _ _ _ _ _

God miraculously parted the river for Elisha to cross. Just as He had done for Elijah (v14).

3

_ _ _ _ _ _ _ _

The prophets said that Elijah's spirit was resting on Elisha (v15).

The prophets didn't really believe that Elijah had gone to heaven, so they sent out a search party! (v16-18) They found no one, because Elijah really had gone.

THINK+PRAY

Do you ever think about **heaven**? The Bible tells us that <u>everyone</u> who trusts in Jesus will one day live with Him in heaven. We don't know when or how we'll go (although it probably won't be in a chariot of fire like Elijah!). But we do know it will be <u>great</u>, because Jesus has promised to prepare a special place for us. *(That promise is in John 14v2.)* If you're a follower of Jesus, you can look forward to being in heaven with Him. How does that make you feel? Talk to Him about it now.

TIME FOR MORE?

Have you read all 65 days of XTB?
Well done if you have!

How often do you use XTB?
- Every day?
- Nearly every day?
- Two or three times a week?
- Now and then?

You can use XTB at any time...

In the morning.

At bedtime.

When you get back from school.

When do <u>you</u> read XTB?

XTB comes out every three months. If you've been using it every day, or nearly every day, that's great! You may still have a few weeks to wait before you get the next issue of XTB. But don't worry!—that's what the extra readings are for...

EXTRA READINGS
The next four pages contain extra Bible readings from the book of Proverbs. If you read one each day, they will take you 26 days. Or you may want to read two or three each day. Or just pick a few to try. Whichever suits you best. There's a cracking wordsearch to solve too...

Drop us a line...
Why not write in and tell us what you think of XTB:
—What do you like best?
—Was there something you didn't understand?
—And any ideas for how we can make it better!

Write to: XTB, The Good Book Company, 37 Elm Road, New Malden, Surrey, KT3 3HB
or e-mail me:
alison@thegoodbook.co.uk

The extra readings start on the next page

SOLOMON'S PROVERBS

As we saw on Day 17, God gave King Solomon the gift of **wisdom**. Solomon wrote the book of Proverbs to show us that loving and obeying God is the <u>wisest</u> way to live...

Proverbs

Proverbs are short sayings full of wisdom. They often tell us what <u>isn't</u> wise as well as what <u>is</u>. You may find that these proverbs include some words you don't understand. If so, ask an older Christian to help you, or look them up in a dictionary.

The ideas in the box will help you as you read the verses.

PRAY Ask God to help you to understand what you read.

READ Read the Bible verses, and fill in the missing word in the puzzle.

THINK Think about what you have just read. Try to work out one main thing the writer is saying.

PRAY Thank God for what you have learnt about Him.

There are 26 Bible readings on the next three pages. Part of each reading has been printed for you—but with a word missing. Fill in the missing words as you read the verses. Then see if you can find them all in the wordsearch below. Some are written backwards—or diagonally!

If you get stuck, check the answers at the end of Reading 26.

K	O	F	A	T	H	E	R	S	Y	T	G	X	D	N
G	N	S	R	E	H	T	O	M	Z	O	E	T	I	O
E	C	O	M	P	A	R	E	J	A	M	N	B	A	M
N	E	A	W	I	S	D	O	M	L	O	T	T	R	O
E	A	P	E	L	T	S	P	O	O	R	L	S	F	L
R	R	T	O	W	E	R	E	A	V	R	E	E	A	O
O	T	X	T	B	A	D	U	C	E	O	L	N	F	S
U	H	F	I	G	O	D	G	S	S	W	O	O	R	X
S	S	N	E	T	S	I	L	E	T	G	R	H	I	T
T	U	N	E	H	O	N	O	U	R	I	D	S	E	B
R	I	C	H	D	R	O	W	S	O	V	K	I	N	G
V	E	G	E	T	A	B	L	E	S	E	O	D	D	S

Tick the box when you have read the verses.

Chapter One

1 ☐ **Read Proverbs 1v1-6**

The book of Proverbs was written by King Solomon. He wrote Proverbs to give wisdom and understanding.

'The proverbs of **S** _ _ _ _ _ _ son of David, the king of Israel.' (v1)

2 ☐ **Read Proverbs 1v7**

To 'fear' God doesn't mean being scared of Him! It means to love and respect God, and to show it by obeying Him. Solomon says that this is 'the beginning of knowledge'.

'The fear of the LORD is the beginning of **k** _ _ _ _ _ _ _ _ _ .' (v7) (Note: Some Bible versions say 'reverence' instead of 'fear'.)

3 ☐ **Read Proverbs 1v8-9**

Solomon tells us to listen to what our parents teach us, and not forget it!

' Listen to your **f** _ _ _ _ _ _ ' teaching, and do not forget your **m** _ _ _ _ _ _ ' advice.' (v8)

4 ☐ **Read Proverbs 1v10-19**

Sometimes other people will try to get you to disobey God (to sin). Don't give in to them!

'When sinners tempt you, do not **g** _ _ _ in to them.' (v10)

5 ☐ **Read Proverbs 1v20-27**

Solomon writes about 'wisdom' as if she is a person, calling out to people and warning them not to ignore her.

' **W** _ _ _ _ _ _ calls aloud in the street, she raises her voice in the public squares.' (v20)

6 ☐ **Read Proverbs 1v28-33**

Solomon warns us of the dangers of ignoring 'wisdom', but then tells us that listening to 'wisdom' (and doing what she says) is the way to be safe, and not afraid.

'Whoever **l** _ _ _ _ _ _ _ to me will be safe, with no reason to be afraid.' (v33)

Chapter Three

7 ☐ **Read Proverbs 3v1-4**

If we are loving, kind and truthful, then we will please both God and other people.

'Then you will be respected and pleasing to both **G** _ _ and men.' (v4)

8 ☐ **Read Proverbs 3v5-6**

God's ways are always best, so we should trust and obey Him—not just do what we think is best.

'**T** _ _ _ _ in the LORD with all your heart. Don't depend on your own understanding.' (v5)

9 ☐ **Read Proverbs 3v7-10**

Solomon told the people to give God the best of what they owned. For them, that often meant the crops they grew. What could it be for you? (Your money? Your time? The things you're good at?).

'**H** _ _ _ _ _ the LORD with your wealth.' (v9)

10 ☐ **Read Proverbs 3v11-12**

Parents who love their children don't ignore the wrong things they do. They correct them ('discipline' them) to help them change and grow up. God does the same thing.

'The LORD disciplines (corrects) those He l _ _ _ _ .' (v12)

11 ☐ **Read Proverbs 3v13-18**

Living by God's wisdom is far better than having money and jewels!

'Wisdom is more valuable than jewels; nothing you want could c _ _ _ _ _ _ with her.' (v15)

12 ☐ **Read Proverbs 3v19-20**

God created our world, and everything in it, by His great wisdom.

'The LORD created the e _ _ _ _ by His wisdom.' (v19)

13 ☐ **Read Proverbs 3v21-26**

Living God's way is <u>always</u> the best. If we do, we never need to be afraid.

'You will not be a _ _ _ _ _ when you go to bed.' (v24)

14 ☐ **Read Proverbs 3v27-35**

If you're able to help someone, don't put it off, do it straight away.

'Never tell your neighbour to wait until t _ _ _ _ _ _ _ _ if you can help him now.' (v28)

Living God's way

15 ☐ **Read Proverbs 10v4-5**

If you're lazy, you'll lose out.

'Being l _ _ _ will make you poor.' (v4)

16 ☐ **Read Proverbs 10v26**

Don't be lazy. It's as irritating as drinking vinegar!!!

'A lazy man will be as irritating as v _ _ _ _ _ _ _ on your teeth or smoke in your eyes.' (v26)

17 ☐ **Read Proverbs 11v1**

God hates it when we cheat others.

'The LORD hates d _ _ _ _ _ _ _ _ _ scales, but accurate weights are His delight.' (v1)

18 ☐ **Read Proverbs 11v24-25**

Giving things away <u>doesn't</u> mean we end up with nothing. Generous people are given a lot back.

'Be g _ _ _ _ _ _ _ _ , and you will be prosperous. Help others, and you will be helped.' (v25)

19 ☐ **Read Proverbs 12v17-19**

Be careful how you use words, so that you help people rather than hurting them.

'Thoughtless words can wound as deeply as any **s** _ _ _ _ but wisely spoken words can heal.' (v18)

20 ☐ **Read Proverbs 15v1-2**

If someone is angry with you, don't shout at them. Answer quietly and gently, to calm them down.

'A **g** _ _ _ _ _ _ answer quietens anger, but a harsh one stirs it up.' (v1)

21 ☐ **Read Proverbs 15v16-17**

It's better to be with people you love, and who love God, even if they are poor, than to be with rich people who don't care about you.

'Better to eat **v** _ _ _ _ _ _ _ _ _ _ with people you love than to eat the finest meat where there is hate.' (v17)

22 ☐ **Read Proverbs 17v17**

Being a good friend means loving and helping your friends at <u>all</u> times (good as well as bad). Who can you be a good friend to today?

'A **f** _ _ _ _ _ _ loves at all times.' (v17)

God is the Real King

23 ☐ **Read Proverbs 18v10**

God is like a strong tower. If we trust in Him, He will keep us safe.

'The name of the LORD is a strong **t** _ _ _ _ .' (v10)

24 ☐ **Read Proverbs 19v21**

God is the Real King. His plans <u>always</u> work out.

'People may plan all kinds of things, but the **L** _ _ _ 's will is going to be done.' (v21)

25 ☐ **Read Proverbs 21v1-3**

Kings and Presidents might seem powerful—but it's <u>God</u> who's really in control!

'The LORD controls the mind (heart) of a **k** _ _ _ as easily as He directs the course of a stream.' (v1)

26 ☐ **Read Proverbs 22v2**

God made all of us. He is our Maker, our loving Father and our King.

'The **r** _ _ _ and the **p** _ _ _ _ have this in common: the LORD is the Maker of them all.' (v2)

Answers:

1 Solomon, 2 Knowledge, 3 Father's & Mother's, 4 Give, 5 Wisdom, 6 Listens, 7 God, 8 Trust, 9 Honour, 10 Loves, 11 Compare, 12 Earth, 13 Afraid, 14 Tomorrow, 15 Lazy, 16 Vinegar, 17 Dishonest, 18 Generous, 19 Sword, 20 Gentle, 21 Vegetables, 22 Friend, 23 Tower, 24 LORD's, 25 King, 26 Rich & Poor.

WHAT NEXT?

XTB comes out every three months. Each issue contains 65 full XTB pages, plus 26 days of extra readings. By the time you've used them all, the next issue of XTB will be available.

ISSUE ELEVEN OF XTB
Issue Eleven of XTB explores the books of John, 2 Kings, Isaiah and Jeremiah.
- The Gospel of **John** tells us all about Jesus. Read about some more of the miracles that pointed to <u>who</u> Jesus is.
- Read about the last kings of Israel, and how the Israelites had to leave their homes, in the books of **2 Kings, Isaiah** and **Jeremiah**.

Available March 2005 from your local Christian bookshop —or call us on **0845 225 0880** to order a copy.

Look out for these three seasonal editions of XTB: *Christmas Unpacked, Easter Unscrambled* and *Summer Signposts*. Available now.

XTB Joke Page

Why did the golfer wear two pairs of pants?
In case he got a hole in one!
Katie Chester

Where does flying fruit land?
At the pearport!
Jenny Thornborough

Why were the Egyptian children confused?
Because their daddies were mummies!

What is a snowman's favourite cereal?
Frosties!

Doctor, Doctor, I feel like a dustbin!
Stop talking rubbish!

What do you get if you cross a camel and a cow? Lumpy custard!

All sent in by Joanna and Emily Fawcett

What did the grape say when it got squashed?
Nothing, it just gave a little wine!

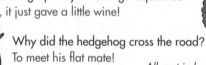

Why did the hedgehog cross the road?
To meet his flat mate!

What do you call a pig with three eyes?
A piiig!

All sent in by James Dawson

Do <u>you</u> know any good jokes?
—send them in and they might appear in XTB!

Do you have any questions?
...about anything you've read in XTB?
—send them in and we'll do our best to answer them.

Write to: XTB, The Good Book Company, 37 Elm Road, New Malden, Surrey, KT3 3HB **or e-mail me:** alison@thegoodbook.co.uk